DEVOTIONS
FROM THE
Garden

DEVOTIONS
FROM THE
Garden

Dr. Delicia Walker

ISBN 978-1-957582-83-2 (paperback)
ISBN 978-1-957582-82-5 (eBook)

Printed in the United States of America

WESTPOINT
PRINT AND MEDIA

Dear Reader,

DEVOTIONS from the GARDEN
will provide tranquil awareness
and remind you of God's
spiritual presence and bring
inspiration, relaxation, and
peace to your daily life.

Dedication

To those seeking peace and tranquility
in their lives, trust and depend on
God. Approach God with a humble
spirit and align your desires with
His will. Surrender to Him and
give honor and glory for blessings
and answered prayers. Develop a
consistent prayer life, recognize God's
presence, and focus upon Him!

Introduction

Pray without ceasing.
1 Thessalonians 5:17 KJV

God loves you. He cares about you deeply and is concerned about your daily life. Everything about you brings joy and a smile to His face.

Because God cares for you, rest assured you can love Him with all your heart. The Bible tells us to pray repeatedly and how those prayers will be answered.

God loves his children. God values our commitment to Him and will guide us toward godliness. God wants us to develop a lifestyle that is pleasing to Him and a relationship that is fruitful to enjoy.

Garden Poem

To Plant
a Garden
is to Believe
in Tomorrow

~Audrey Hepburn

Feel closer
to God in
the garden
by inspired
garden imagery
and pictures
featuring
scripture and
storytelling
to uplift and
motivate those
who enjoy
spending quality
time outdoors.

Take your devotion to the next level by connecting more with God, strengthening your relationship with Him. Identify areas in your life spiritually and complete activities that correspond. Then, schedule time to do ministry.

How Do You View Yourself?

An Ugly View of Yourself
I am very ugly
So, do not try to convince me that
I am a very beautiful person
Because at the end of the day
I hate myself in every single way
And I am not going to lie to myself by saying
There is beauty inside of me that matters
So, rest assured I will remind myself
That I am a worthless, terrible person
And nothing you say will make me believe
I still deserve love
Because no matter what
I am not good enough to be loved
And I am in no position to believe that
Beauty does exist within me
Because whenever I look in the mirror, I always think
Am I as ugly as people say?
A Pretty View of Yourself
(Same picture, different view. *Read from bottom to top*)

God Is Our Refuge

God is our refuge and strength, a very present help in trouble.
Psalm 46:1 KJV

Whenever you face daunting and disturbing situations, you have a refuge. For instance, a phone call that brings bad news or you experience a physical pain in your body, you can call upon God for help and strength. Seek God during these moments of difficulties and pray for solitude and rest in His arms.

He Is Always Ours

Let your conversation be without covetousness; and be content with such things as ye have: for he hath said, I will never leave thee, nor forsake thee.

Hebrew 13:5 KJV

God is eternal.
His love, grace, and mercy are unchanging.
When we allow God to be the center of our lives, we can rest assure that He is always with us,
keeping His hands on us.
What an amazing testament!

Heaven on Earth

*Thy kingdom come, Thy will be done
in earth, as it is in heaven.*
Matthew 6:10 KJV

God involves us in His daily plans
on earth. He has great plans for us
through our supplication of prayers.
His desire for you is to exercise your
faith and strength in His will. Our
prayers grant us access to God in
heaven as He is generous. Seek boldly
the kingdom of heaven and pray to
God to make your request happen.

God Is Merciful

But God, who is rich in mercy, for his great love wherewith he loved us, Even when we were dead in sins, hath quickened us together with Christ, (by grace ye are saved;) And hath raised us up together, and made us sit together in heavenly places in Christ Jesus:
Ephesians 2:4-6 KJV

We are not deserving of God's love, yet God sees us worthy through His Son who sacrificed His life for us. God forgives us of our sins repeatedly. God opens the door for us to come to Him despite our transgressions and gives us a pathway to freedom. By God's grace and mercy, we can strive for holiness and become more like Him.

Embrace New Beginnings

Verily, verily, I say unto you, Except a corn of wheat fall into the ground and die, it abideth alone: but if it die, it bringeth forth much fruit.
John 12:24 KJV

Planting seeds produce a plentiful harvest. In the same manner, there is a season for everything under heaven. When we do things that glorify God and give him praise, we blossom like harvest and spring forth new vines. A smile, an encouraging word, a phone call, and a visit to a friend all can have a lasting impact to someone's life and give them hope.

Timing

He hath made every thing beautiful in his time:
also he hath set the world in their heart, so
that no man can find out the work that God
maketh from the beginning to the end.
Ecclesiastes 3:11 KJV

Timing is a slow process and can be frustrating waiting on others. Timing is an indicator that God is in control and trusting in His timing reap a beautiful blessing far beyond what you can imagine. God is directing our steps. At the right time, He will supply all your needs. We do not always understand God's actions, but we can trust Him and wait for Him and know that your day will come.

Live in the Spirit

But ye are not in the flesh, but in the Spirit, if so be that the Spirit of God dwell in you. Now if any man have not the Spirit of Christ, he is none of his.
Romans 8:9 KJV

Having a defeatist attitude allows for setbacks and disappointments. Embracing a winning attitude develops a positive spirit and mindset. Set your eyes on the prize and conquer the challenge. God has given you a new life. God wants you in His divine spirit. Cross the finish line, claim the victory, and proclaim, I Win!

Agreement

Again I say unto you, That if two of you shall agree on earth as touching any thing that they shall ask, it shall be done for them of my Father which is in heaven.
Matthew 18:19 KJV

There is power in the name of Jesus. When two or more people gather and join forces in prayer, they unleash a greater power in the Lord's presence. Prayer is limitless. Draw nearer in the presence of God and agree together that prayers will be answered. Focus on God's will and trust Him.

Solving Everyone's Problems

*And let us consider one another to provoke
unto love and to good works:*
Hebrews 10:24 KJV

Oftentimes, people think their way is the best and how everyone should listen and adhere to it. People have different responses. Taking on that position seems unrealistic. Solving everyone's problems is not a matter or requirement. You cannot force anyone to accept God, but you can encourage people to seek Him. Bring your situation to God and allow Him to make the situation better. Only prayer can alter the situation. Thank God for all that He has done.

Rest

Come unto me, all ye that labour and are heavy laden, and I will give you rest.

Take my yoke upon you, and learn of me; for I am meek and lowly in heart: and ye shall find rest unto your souls.

For my yoke is easy, and my burden is light.
Matthew 11:28-30 KJV

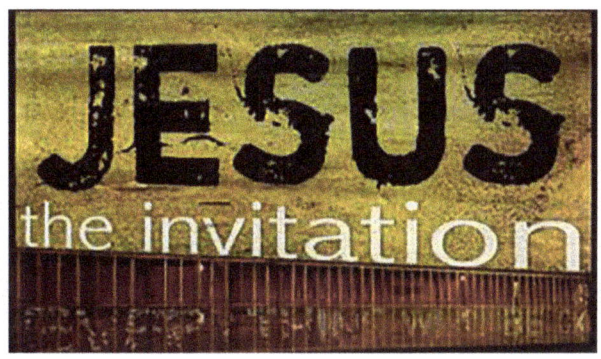

Do you find yourself exhausted and fatigued because of too many tasks with little time to complete? Remember where your strength come from. Ask God to show you how to rest and prioritize your day accordingly. Live freely and recover your life for peaceful tranquility and vitality.

God Is Our Healer

Suffering from recurring health challenges can be miserable. Consulting with the doctor can yield the decision for administering prescription medication or surgery. Praying about the situation is necessary for deciding a decision. Surely, God, the Great Physician, can provide an answer. God can make the pain subside and heal your body.

God
Is
Available

Setting aside quiet time every morning for devotion draws us close to God. Make yourself available to read the Bible. God is flexible. Expand your Christian faith. Read this devotional while waiting in transition. Stay focused on the goal you set and allow God to penetrate your thoughts and conversations. Whatever you do, keep God in the center of all things and strengthen your relationship with Him. By God's grace, you can grow closer to Him and live out His greater plan.

Tribulation

Look Up

And when these things
begin to come to pass,
then look up, and lift
up your heads; for your
redemption draweth nigh.
Luke 21:28 KJV

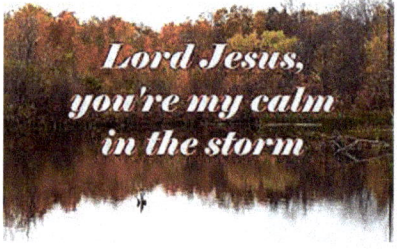

This world is filled with natural disasters, world health crisis, global pandemics, and dangerous crimes that can impact our lives with fear and anxiety. When I find myself consumed by these negative circumstances, I look to God for strength. God, the Creator of all things, knows what is going on in this world and will keep us safe from harm and danger.

Live Your Life Spiritually

Holiness is what we all need and strive for. God wants us to transform our mind to be molded to be like Him for His will and righteousness. Holiness is what God wants for you and me.

Be a generous *Giver.*
God will BLESS you more *abundantly.*

*Give from
your heart....
for God loves
a cheerful
giver!*

2 Corinthians 9:7

Thou wilt shew me the path of life: in thy presence is fulness of joy; at thy right hand there are pleasures for evermore.
Psalm 16:11 KJV

You have made known to me
the path of life;
in your presence there is
fullness of joy.

Psalm 16:11

God made all things beautiful. All around
us are beautiful blessings. Take notice
of all nature and grow closer to God.

And why take ye thought for raiment?
Consider the lilies of the field, how they
grow; they toil not, neither do they spin:
Matthew 6:28 KJV

Give Thanks and Praise God!

*Draw nigh to God, and he will draw nigh
to you. Cleanse your hands, ye sinners; and
purify your hearts, ye double minded.*
James 4:8 KJV

AND	CLEANSE	CLOSE
COME	DRAW	GOD
HANDS	HEARTS	JOY
NEAR	PURIFY	SINNERS
TO	WILL	YOU

Blessings appear as we learn
patience and wait on God,
trusting Him to work in our lives.

Grant me
patience
to deal with my
blessings

Worry can sprout up like weeds and control our thoughts and feelings and consume all our time. But if we recognize and face our fears, we can take comfort knowing that God will weed out our fears and plant seeds that will ripe and flourish.

"I've had a lot of worries in my life, most of which never happened."
- Mark Twain

Grace

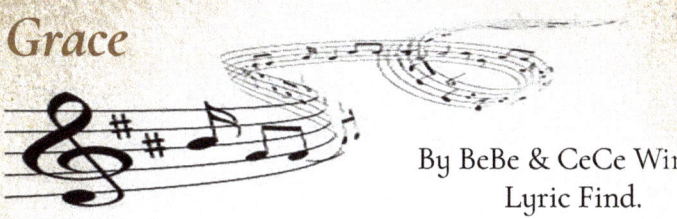

By BeBe & CeCe Winans
Lyric Find.

Heaven knows I've done wrong; mercy helped me see I've been living a lie.
And while writing this song, thinking 'bout Your goodness I started to cry.
Yes, oh oh oh grace; what would I do without grace (do without grace)

Hide behind a painted smile; you lash out and sing while you're
spiritually down, yeah
There's no need to sit in denial; He knows all about it and understands
why (yes He does)
Oh oh oh grace (oh grace oh grace); what would I do without grace
Oh oh oh grace; where would I be, where would I be without grace

How can you love me still when I've done wrong (grace)
And how can I make it through this angry storm (oh grace)
Say oh oh oh grace; what would I do without Your grace
Oh oh oh grace; where would I be without grace (where would I be
without grace)

What can make me whole in my soul (grace grace)
What can wash my sin (grace)
Say grace; what would I do without Your grace (couldn't make it)

Tell you what lately I've learned; He picks me up whenever I'm down
(Have you ever been down? I've been down.)
Nothin' I've done or can do can take away this love, this love that I've found

Oh oh oh grace (grace); what would I do, what would I do without grace
Oh oh oh grace; where would I be without grace

Amazing grace how sweet the sound that saved a wretch like me
I once was lost but now I'm found, I was blind but now I see

That's why we say amazing; that's why we sing amazing grace (I can't
move without it)
I can't live without Your grace; thank You for Your grace

GOD'S GRACE IS SUFFICIENT TO MEET ALL OUR NEEDS.

Being a gardener is essential for cultivating out a place for planting, watering, and weeding.

God is planting seeds in us full of life and joy for a bountiful harvest.

Don't be impressed by:
1. Money
2. Followers
3. Degrees
4. Titles

Be impressed by:
1. Generosity
2. Integrity
3. Humility
4. Kindness

No matter what
happens in life,
keep a
good heart.
A heart of
patience & trust.
Don't let the
darkness of this
world harden
your

heart.

Peace

Thou wilt keep him in perfect peace, whose mind is stayed on thee: because he trusteth in thee. **Isaiah 26:3 KJV**

On a recent vacation trip to my family, I was sleeping in the guest room. I laid in the bed for thirty minutes, but I was not sleeping. I was resting consumed in thoughts about the plans for the day. I also meditated on God's Word realizing I was safe and secure. God's immeasurable peace radiated all around me. Find a place where you can rest in His presence knowing that you will encounter peace there.

Self-Control

But the Holy Spirit produces this kind of fruit in our lives: love, joy, peace, patience, kindness, goodness, faithfulness, gentleness, and self-control. There is no law against these things! **Galatians 5:22-23 NLT**

Self-control requires daily discipline. As we grow in our spiritual walk, God helps us with selfish desires and indulgences. For example, you ponder over whether to eat an unhealthy snack, or engage in an exercise regime. God directs our attention to stay focused on Him and not ourselves!

Christian believers plant seeds of knowledge that will grow forever.

God Is Forever

For all flesh is as grass, and all the glory of man as the flower of grass.
The grass withereth, and the flower thereof falleth away:
But the word of the Lord endureth for ever.
And this is the word which by the gospel is preached unto you.

1 Peter 1:24-25 KJV

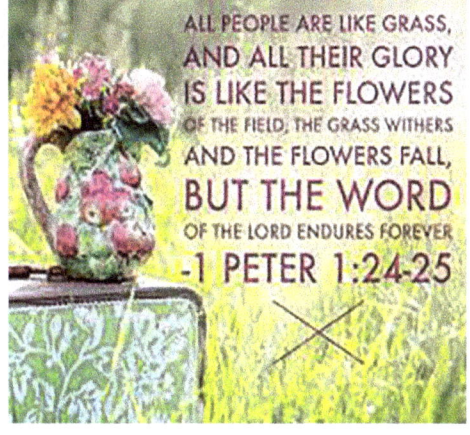

God is eternal and everlasting.
God has no beginning and no end.
He is the author and finisher.
God's word is true forever.
What a blessing and promise from our Lord!
Everything about God is love.
He will never leave us nor forsake us.
Hold on to God's unchanging hand!

God Is Holy

But as he which hath called you is holy,
so be ye holy in all manner of conversation.
Because it is written, Be ye holy;
for I am holy.
1 Peter 1:15-16 KJV

God is without blame.
Meditating on God's Word can increase your faith and shift your focus and direction of holiness.
God is perfect in every way.
By God's grace, you can strengthen your knowledge and understanding by acknowledging His holiness to become more like Him.

God Is Our Friend

And the scripture was fulfilled which saith, Abraham believed God, and it was imputed unto him for righteousness: and he was called the Friend of God.
James 2:23 KJV

God is available to hear our secrets, thoughts, and concerns. We can give thanks and praise Him for all of life blessings. It is so amazing to know that we can approach God to include Him in our life's journey, pray to Him in time of need, and trust Him in All things. God is, and will always be, our friend!

To Be Loved

That Christ may dwell in your hearts by faith;
that ye, being rooted and grounded in love,
Ephesians 3:17 KJV

God shows us Agape love. Sometimes that love is hard to accept. However, reflecting on our wrongdoings, faults, and transgressions, we assume that we are unforgiving to be loved. To be honest, God loves us unconditionally. No matter what the cost- whether at our best or worst, we can live our lives freely to be loved by Him.

Embrace You

*Wherefore receive ye one another, as Christ
also received us to the glory of God.*
Romans 15:7 KJV

Have you ever noticed people's behavior embodies
their personality? For instance, if you speak to
someone who does not acknowledge your greeting,
would you ignore them or attempt to illicit a
response? People may not be aware of their obvious
mannerisms. Whether intentional or subdued,

God accepts you for who you are.

Stand Out

Ephesians 3:16 KJV
That he would grant you, according to the riches of his glory, to be strengthened with might by his Spirit in the inner man;

Sometimes God calls upon us to speak truth to the world, whether through social media, personal contact, or other means of communication. Oftentimes, speaking truth requires hearing from God and seeking discernment and His direction. Whenever you are facing something that is outside of your comfort zon00e, drawing strength from God is paramount as His glory and power fuels the energy in one's life.

"Always speak the truth. No matter what."

Patience

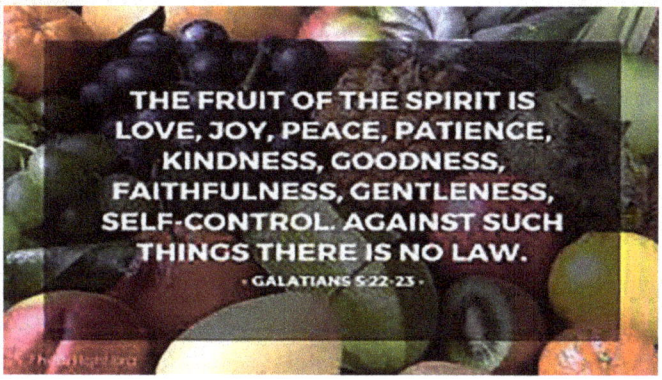

Too often at church, I notice that people are distracted by technology-the use of cell phones and tablets. When this happens, impatience and unfocused dominates and God no longer becomes the center of devotion. When we allow God's spirit to reside within, we strengthen our patience, and listen and focus on God's Word.

That Christ may dwell in your hearts by faith;
that ye, being rooted and grounded in love,
Ephesians 3:17 KJV

I feel overjoyed when everything is going "right" in my life. I also have the same sentiment when life becomes too difficult to manage. Thoughts of worry and fear attempt to settle, but I reject those feelings. We can trust God through every area in our life and moments of difficulty and live in peace. We can be content knowing that we are at peace.

Be Courageous

Have you ever noticed trash debris on the ground that people walked by and chose not to pick up? Probably, people did not want to do something unusual to be noticed.

God wants us to be different from everyone else and make a difference in the lives of others. In other words, God is calling upon us to be bold thinkers and courageous people in the world. Being courageous allows for God to move in our lives and create spiritual change.

Have not I commanded thee? Be strong and of a good courage; be not afraid, neither be thou dismayed: for the LORD thy God is with thee whithersoever thou goest.

Joshua 1:9 KJV

Christian One Liners

one-liner

People are kind, polite, and sweet-
spirited until you sit in their pews.
God didn't create things without purpose,
but mosquitoes come close.
Quit griping about your church; if it
were perfect, you couldn't belong.
We are called to be witnesses, not lawyers or Judges.
Minds are like concrete thoroughly
mixed up and permanently set.
Why do people change churches; what difference
does it make which one you stay home from?
Be ye fishers of men. you catch 'em and God will clean 'em.
Stop, Drop, and Roll will not work in Hell.
Do not put a question mark where God put a period.
Forbidden fruits create many jams.
God doesn't call the qualified, He qualifies the called.
God loves everyone but prefers 'fruit of
the spirit' over 'religious nuts!'
If God is your Co-pilot, swap seats!
Don't change the Word of God. Let
the Word of God change you.
The best mathematical equation ever:
1 cross + 3 nails = 4 given.

God's Spirit

Fruit trees bear fruit. Planting seeds is required for growing fruit. As long as fruit stays connected to the tree, they will grow and produce plenty fruit.

Likewise, when we stay connected to God's purpose and grow in the Spirit, we bear the **fruit** of the Spirit outlined in Galatians chapter 5.

I Love You More

When I say I love you More,
I don't mean I love you more than you love me.
I mean I love you more than the bad days ahead of us.
I love you **more** than any fight we will ever have.
I love you *more* than the distance between us.
I love you more than any obstacle that
could try and come between us.
I love you the Most!!!

Greek Words for Love

Eros - romantic love.
Storge -family love.
Philia – brotherly love.
Agape –unconditional love.

He that loveth not knoweth not God; for God is love.
1 John 4:8 KJV

HEAVEN'S GROCERY STORE

By: Power Poetry

I was walking down life's
highway a long time ago.
One day I saw a sign that read,
"Heaven's Grocery Store".
As I got a little closer the
door came open wide,
and when I came to myself
I was standing inside.
I saw a host of Angels, they
were standing everywhere.
One handed me a blanket and
said, "My Child shop with care".
Everything a Christian
needs is in that grocery store,
and all you can't carry, come back the next day for more.
First, I got some Patience, Love was in the same row.
Further down was Understanding,
needed everywhere you go.
I got a box or two of Wisdom, a bag or two of Faith,
I just couldn't miss the Holy Ghost,
it was all over the place.
I stopped to get some Strength and
Courage to help me run this race,
but then my blanket was getting full, and
I remembered I needed Grace.
I didn't forget Salvation, which like the others was free,
so I tried to get enough of that to save both you and me.
Then I started to the counter to pay my grocery bill,
for I thought I had everything to do my master's will.
As I went up the aisle, I saw Prayer and had to put it in,
for I knew when I stepped outside,
I would run right into sin.
Peace and Joy were plentiful, they were on the last shelf.

49

Song and Praises were hanging near, so I just helped
myself.
Then I said to the Angel, "How much do I owe"?
The Angel smiled and said, "Just take
them everywhere you go."
Again, I politely asked "How much do I really owe?"
The Angel smiled again
and said, "My Child,
Jesus Paid Your Bill
A Long Time Ago."

*I had to memorize and recite
this poem as a child at my
grandmother's church.*

Fruit of the Spirit

22 But the fruit of the
Spirit is love, joy, peace,
longsuffering, gentleness,
goodness, faith,
23 Meekness, temperance:
against such there is no law.

Galatians 5:22-23 KJV

Mediterranean Greek Salad

Prep **20** MIN   Total **20** MIN   Servings **8**

Lemon Dressing
¼ cup vegetable oil
2 tablespoons lemon juice
½ teaspoon sugar
1 ½ teaspoons Dijon mustard
¼ teaspoon salt
1/8 teaspoon pepper

Salad
7 oz spinach, torn into bite-size pieces (5 cups)
1 head Boston lettuce, torn into bite-size pieces (4 cups)
1 package (4 oz) crumbled feta cheese (1 cup)
4 medium green onions, sliced (1/4 cup)
24 pitted ripe olives
3 medium tomatoes, cut into wedges
1 medium cucumber, sliced

THOUGHTS

If my people, which are called by my name, shall humble themselves, and pray, and seek my face, and turn from their wicked ways; then will I hear from heaven, and will forgive their sin, and will heal their land.
2 Chronicles 7:14 KJV

> SNOOPY, MANY FOLKS ARE PRAYING FOR GOD TO HEAL OUR LAND, BUT I THINK HE'S STILL WAITING FOR PEOPLE TO HUMBLE THEMSELVES, REPENT AND TURN FROM THEIR WICKED WAYS.

Be Considerate

*Let every one of us please his neighbour
for his good to edification.*
Romans 15:2 KJV

Before I post messages on social media, I ask myself Why am I posting this? If it is to boast, brag, or stir controversy, then it is all in vain. **When I post something,** I want the message to be truthful, thoughtful, meaningful, and encouraging to others. I want to **bring awareness and spiritual understanding to others. Being thoughtful and considerate** involves thinking of others first.

Clothed in Love

*Above all, clothe yourselves with love, which
binds us all together in perfect harmony.*
Colossians 3:14 NLT

*Clothing is essential for daily wear. It protects us from
the harsh elements. Clothing gives us the confidence to
boldly step out into the world to approach the day. In
the same manner, expressions of love ensure confidence,
protection, and a stronger connection to God. Put your
love garments on today!*

FLOWERS

```
M T B E G J F J I N R O L K P
P T C P V A R R W F G L B P C
E E A H O Y S N P J J M V E I
T K R W L P B L F F M L T O M
U I N T P W P V T A K A U N P
N G A O S X M Y G Z T N L Y A
I A T G E R A N I U M T I W T
A R I G L O W I L P L A P R I
L D O R O S E Y M K W N S Y E
L E N K V C V M H A P A R G N
I N D A H L I A T M E K L R S
L I A I S X B E G O N I A R I
Y A S F M L Q H I B I S C U S
Z X I H Y D R A N G E A F L V
I U Z A P A R L Q C R B A C N
```

CARNATION	HYDRANGEA	GARDENIA	GERANIUM
BEGONIA	HIBISCUS	PETUNIA	IMPATIENS
LANTANA	TULIPS	DAHLIA	POPPY
PEONY	ROSE	LILY	

Reflection Notes

A Beautiful Garden Is Coming

Gardens are a great example that we reap what we sow. Starting from the Garden of Eden that God provided for Adam and Eve, to gardens we create and maintain today providing food and beauty.

I made me gardens and orchards, and I planted trees in them of all kind of fruits:
Ecclesiastes 2:5 KJV

PRAYER & MEDITATION

Prayer is when you talk to God,

meditation is when you listen to God.
-Unknown

God has given us the authority in prayer. Give God the opportunity to be the center-focus in your life.

Think about something that makes you a better person. Meditation can be good for your health. This practice can help you focus, become centered, reduce stress, and regulate efficient sleep.

And the LORD shall guide thee continually, and satisfy thy soul in drought, and make fat thy bones: and thou shalt be like a watered garden, and like a spring of water, whose waters fail not.
Isaiah 58:11 KJV

Faith Journey

It's more than a destination.

Thank you for all your support. I am grateful and appreciative for your kindness and generosity and heartfelt expressions of joy. I want to extend a special thank you to the reader, my mother Sheila Farquharson, grandparents; Wilhelmena Farquharson(deceased), Uellen Williams, family, and friends and to my husband Pastor Anthony Walker for being a spiritual adviser, confidant, and friend in Christ Jesus. I pray for peace and happiness as your heart and soul blossom.

With gratitude and grace,
Dr. Delicia Walker

About the Author

Dr. Delicia Walker is a writer, author, mentor, business professional, and a woman of faith. Her spiritual calling is to encourage, motivate, and inspire others. Dr. Walker's spiritual foundation in ministry has taken her through real life experiences, and reveals powerful testimonies through counseling of others, guidance, and her writings.

Delicia has also written the following books:

"Today You Are Loved," *and "Blessings And Peaceful Promises."*

Devotions From The Garden